Keisha "B

Been Released

Overcome * Transformed * Set Free
"I Will Overcome Be Strong
And Keep On Keeping On"

Keisha "Been Released" Wade

Keisha "Been Released" Wade

Copyright © 2020 by Keisha L. Wade

All Rights Reserved.

No part of this book may be reproduced, scanned, or distributed in any manner whatsoever without permission in writing from the author, except in a case of brief quotation embodied in critical passages, articles and reviews.

DEDICATION

First I want to give Honor to God who is the head of my life. I dedicate this book to my husband, children, family and friends that have supported me through everything. I truly appreciate you all!

Message from Keisha "Been Released"

My life is in God's hands. Have you ever felt like given up? If so, I know how you feel. I truly thank God because He gives me the strength to keep going and to have Faith in Him. As I continue to have Faith and Trust in God, I overcame to come over to what God had in store for me. I want to encourage you that you can overcome hurt, pain, trails, tribulations, and the situation that you are going through right now. Remember, there is nothing too hard for GOD. I am Keisha "Been Released", and some people may ask why I encourage others, and I say I have a story to tell and it's Ministry in me. In spite of all my trials and tribulations, I have been broken to Minister. I'm a vessel that God has chosen to use to encourage His people. God has truly gotten me through situations and by Him getting me through, I must encourage others that they can overcome too, and if God did it for me I know that God will do it for you. I always say "My Past Will Be A Testimony For My Future". I say all of this because, **"I Am An Overcomer"**! God is preparing you, so get ready for your transition move. You are coming out of this situation sooner than you think. You will overcome the situation, and not the situation overcome you. Continue to Pray Believe and Rejoice, because God has already worked it out for you!
~Stay Encouraged~

CONTENTS

About Released 1

I Am An Overcomer
*Overcome *Transformed *Set Free

Chapter 1: Overcome To Testify................................. 4

Chapter 2: Overcome Your Past................................. 6

Chapter 3: Overcome To Forgive............................... 9

Chapter 4: Love and Healing Process....................... 12

Been Released
I Will Overcome Be Strong And Keep On Keeping On

CHAPTER 5: Seek God First..................................... 17

CHAPTER 6: Do It With Confidence........................ 23

CHAPTER 7: Characteristics Of Being Confident 35

CHAPTER 8: Believe Like and Enjoy Yourself........... 42

CHAPTER 9: Remember Your Dream Vision and Purpose... 47

CHAPTER 10: It's Not Over....................................... 51

I Declare I Am Poem... 54

Keisha "Been Released" Wade

Keisha "Been Released" Wade

About Released:
Released an Encouragement Ministry is designed to Pray, Inspire, Uplift, Encourage, Educate and Empower Others.

Mission:
I Will Overcome Be Strong And Keep On Keeping On.

Vision:
I have a Purpose and I will see myself as God sees me. I am Valuable, I have Worth, I am Gifted, I am Talented, I am more than a Conqueror, I have a Great Future, and I Will Live and Walk into My Purpose!

Motto:
Given up is not an option I will Believe and have Faith because God has given me the opportunity to experience so much more!

Scripture:
"Therefore, if any man be in Christ, he is a new creature: old things are passed away behold, all things are become new."
2nd Corinthians 5:17 KJV

Keisha "Been Released" Wade

Released Encouragement Letter

Dear _____,
       (Your Name)

God's desire is for you to be ***Strong, Healed, Bold, Confident, Loved, Delivered, Set Free, and Successful.*** Continue to be confident in all the things that God has given you the ability to do. See yourself as God sees you, and you will know that you are valuable, you have worth, you are gifted, you are talented, you are more than a conqueror, you have a great future, and something good is going to happen to you, because you have a purpose! ~Stay Encouraged~

Characteristics Of Being Confident

1. You Put God First
2. You Pray
3. You Know Your Purpose
4. You Believe In Yourself
5. You Never Give Up
6. You Are Gifted
7. You Promote A Positive Mindset
8. You Set Goals
9. You Take Action
10. You Invest In Yourself

Released Prayer:

    God, I surrender it all to you, everything I give to you, withholding nothing. God, I know where I am right now, that I'm not going to stay there. God, I know that you are going to take me to another level to push me to my Vision and Purpose you have for me. God allow me to be Confident and Bold as you use me to operate in my Vision and My Purpose. God give me a glimpse of Your Vision that you have for my Future, so that I can Understand and Grow according to your Word & Timing. God give me the patience along the way, and the Faith to trust that you are always working for my good. God I just want to thank you for the Confidence that you are giving me to go forward in writing the Vision, Making it Plain, Running with it, and waiting in your timing according to Habakkuk 2:2-3. God, I thank you for what you have done in my life, what you are doing now, and what you are going to do in my future! My Future is Blessed because of you God! I receive every Plan, Promise, and every Blessing that you have for me. In Jesus Name Amen.

Sincerely,
Keisha "Been Released" Wade

I Am An Overcomer

*Overcome * Transformed * Set Free

God is using you to be the change, because it's your testimony that will change someone else's life!

~Stay Encouraged~

Keisha "Been Released" Wade

CHAPTER 1

Overcome To Testify

"Return home and tell [about] all the great things God has done for you." So the man went away, proclaiming throughout the whole city what great things Jesus had done for him."
(Luke 8:39 AMP)

There are many trials and tribulations that you have experienced in your life, and at times you didn't know what to do. I want to remind you that whatever challenges that you are going through, you should always give it to God. When you allow God to lead and guide you through those challenges you will overcome to tell others your testimony. Everybody has a testimony to share, because when you look back over your life and seen where God has brought you from, somebody ought to testify! There's so many things that God has Blessed you with, and brought you out of. When God takes you out of a situation do not return, there is a reason why He took you out of it. Sometimes we go through some experiences because we didn't put God first. You might think that it will be alright, and that's when things start to happen, and then you have a hard time getting out of the situation.

Remember to listen to God's voice so He can lead and guide you, in Proverbs 3:5-6 KJV it says "Trust in the Lord with all thine heart and lean not unto thine own understanding. In all thy ways acknowledge him and he shall direct thy paths." Even thou mistakes have been made or will be made let them be your testimony of life learning

lessons to share with others. Do not be afraid to share your testimony with others. When you share your testimony it will encourage and uplift others that God will get them through it just like He did you. When people look at you, they will know that it wasn't nobody but God that brought you out, because it could have been the other way. Sharing your testimony with others will truly be a blessing because there are so many things that God has done for you. Start sharing your testimony today, so others can see how God took you from Glory to Glory just like He will do for them.
~Stay Encouraged~

Released Encouragement Thought To Remember:
"Share Your Testimony To Encourage Others Through Their Situation."

CHAPTER 2

Overcome Your Past

"For I am the Lord your God who takes hold of your right hand
and says to you, Do not fear; I will help you."
(Isaiah 41:13 NIV)

There are somethings that have happened to you over the past years. Just think about it, is it a person place or thing that you need to overcome from your past? Sometimes you can let your past come into your future. There are somethings that you may have experienced, and it has affected you to where you are today. If something has happened to you then you need to talk about it. Letting things build up inside of you only makes matters worst. When you go through different experiences, you may try to block it out of your mind, but from time to time it somehow comes back in your mind. Some of the things that you may have experienced from your past that may have affected you are domestic violence, molestation, rape, separation, depression, neglect, anger, unforgiveness, verbal abuse, emotional abuse, spiritual abuse and many more. Again, I ask what person, place or thing do you need to overcome from your past? You cannot get through this by yourself. That's why it's great to have someone or some people that you can confide in and talk to. You do not need something that has been built up for so many years to continue to affect you today. In Isaiah 43:18 NIV it states "Forget the former things, do not dwell on the pass". I want to encourage you, and to let you know, that with God you will get through it. Do not continue to let your past or your current situation hinder you or even put a burden on you. Are there somethings that still affect you right now that you need God to Deliver you from? Is there someone that you need to forgive? Don't allow your past to have control over you. If someone has done something to you forgive them. You want to be free from it. Pray Ask and Seek God to help you to overcome from that person place or thing that you are dealing with. God will even send people your way to help you get through it. Give your past or even your current situation to God, because He can handle it better than you can. When you give your situation to God He will give you VICTORY OVER IT!

"Never carry your past to your future you never know what the outcome could be."

Once you have forgiven someone or something that has happened in your past there is no need to keep bringing it back up. If you have brought something up that happened to you in your past, and you are still hurt then you have not really forgiven them or gotten over the situation. When you forgive, it should come from the heart,"…..For the LORD does not see as man sees; for man looks at the outward appearance, but the Lord looks at the heart." (1st Samuel 16:7 NKJV). Continue to be in prayer and pray for God to rebuild, restore, renew, and refresh your mind, heart, body, and spirit. You want to live free and not have all these things to burden you down. "Never carry your pass to your future you never know what the outcome could be." Why

let your past issues mess up your future, your marriage, children or even yourself. Put your situation in the hands of God, and He will fix it for you. There's a cycle that keeps going on, and God can be using you to break that cycle. Once you see that the same situation continues to keep going on, you really need to let go and let God, and let the past simply be the past! God knows that if you try to change it yourself then it will not be done right. Allow God to change you so you can be who He has called you to be. You must remember that God is the source and He gives you the Grace, the Strength, and all the things that you need to do to make changes in your life. Do not worry, because the transition that you are going through, God is going to be right there with you to help you get through it.
~Stay Encouraged~

Released Encouragement Thought To Remember:
"God Will Help You Overcome The Situation, And NOT The Situation Overcome You."

CHAPTER 3

Overcome To Forgive

"Be gentle and ready to forgive; never hold grudges.
Remember, the Lord forgave you,
so you must forgive others."
(Colossians 3:13 TLB)

There are so many different types of issues that you may have experienced in your life such as family, friends, or even relationships. With so many issues or challenges that you have experienced it may have taken a major toll on you. When issues come up always seek God on how to handle a situation. If you do not seek God First, then you will do and say somethings that you may later regret. Always seek God on every decision "But seek ye first the kingdom of God, and his righteousness; and all these things shall be added unto you" (Matthew 6:33 KJV).

When you know a problem or conflict is there, you may have to walk away, remain silent, pray and even seek God before you come back to resolve it. There are going to be some times when you must practice (James 1:19 NIV), "My dear brothers and sisters, take note of this: Everyone should be quick to listen, slow to speak and slow to become angry." You also want to stay calm and humble in 1st Peter 5:6-7 KJV it says, "Humble yourselves therefore under the mighty hand of God, that he may exalt you in due time: Casting all your care upon him; for he careth for you." At this time you should think and realize what's the problem. You then need to pray to Jesus your Savior and ask what or how He wants this situation handled. The bible mentions about love, so if you have an ought with someone then go to them, but go to them in love and not with anger, (Ephesians 4:31-32) (Matthew 5:23-24), (Colossians 3:13), because if you are angry things will not go how it should go. Think about it? What does family, friends, or that relationship that you are in mean to you? Is the issue worth arguing over? When talking the issue out learn to Listen to each other, so the issue can be settled. Reacting and talking too much can cause more issues. Sometimes you can say words to someone that you really don't mean, and then before you know it the situation has went too far.

Also writing how you feel and what the issues are, are a great way for you to express how you maybe feeling. There are some things that disturbs your spirit, it disturbs your peace, and instead of holding on to it, you need to Release it. Holding on to it will only make you feel miserable, angry, depressed, having attitudes for no reason, and the list goes on. Talk with someone or some people that you believe and can confide in, this is a great way to express how you are feeling about the issue. That person(s) can help give you great advice on how to resolve the conflict. Continue to pray to God about how to handle the different issues or challenges that you may face in life. Once you have talked with that person, and you have asked for forgiveness, then just as God do us when we sin, we confess and repent of our sins, and God forgives us. It states in 1st John 1:9 KJV "If we confess our sins, he is faithful and just to forgive us our sins, and to cleanse us from all unrighteousness." At this point it's no need to bring the issue back up. God is saying in order to fully be delivered from this issue you need to release it and give it to Him, so He can fully deliver and set you free you from the issues. Although you may not be around that person all the time it is best to forgive and move on, and start focusing on God, and on the Life He wants you to have! ~Stay Encouraged~

Released Encouragement Thought To Remember:
"Learn To Forgive."

CHAPTER 4

Love and Healing Process

"The LORD is near the brokenhearted; he delivers those who are discouraged." (Psalm 34:18 NET)

You can be smiling on the outside and hurting in the inside, and people will think you are alright. God doesn't want you to walk around feeling hurt, broken, upset or holding on to past hurts, current hurts, this only leaves you feeling hurt inside. The hurt and pain that you feel inside will only keep building things up inside of you and makes matters worse. Talk about it with someone even the strong can break down. Pray and Seek God on all things, because God wants you to Release what's been bothering you to someone, so you can freely move on. God loves you and He wants you to be healed. "He heals the brokenhearted and binds up their wounds" (Psalm 147:3 ESV). There is a process for healing to take place, but you must want God to restore and heal you where you may be hurting. There is something that you went through, and all you can do is cry.

Crying is alright it allows you to release any issues that you may be facing. You must release it and let it go. No one can love or give you the love that God can. When you are in God's presence it's a feeling that will give you peace, joy, comfort, and you will feel at ease. God wants you to love everyone. We can't continue to hold hatred in our hearts. If you hold hatred in your heart you can't function or be fully used by God. He wants to use you. Love and Healing is a process that will take some time to do, but with God leading and guiding you through it, it can be done. God will even send people your way to help you get through it. Ask God to show you who you need to talk to such as family, friends, leaders, mentors, professionals etc.... You want people that will help build you back up to where God wants you to be. This is so you can love, heal, and do all the things that God has planned for your life. Are you ready to let go of all the hurt, brokenness, sadness, bitterness, and most of all, Are You Ready To Forgive? Allow God to come into your heart to heal you, so you can love and enjoy your life. God's word says, "I can do all things through Christ that strengths me" (Philippians 4:13 KJV). God can and will do it for you, all you have to do is be willing to allow God to heal you, so you are able to Feel Love, Give Love, Receive Love and Enjoy Love! ~Stay Encouraged~

"God Heals the broken hearted and binds up their wounds." Psalm 147:3

Released Encouragement Thought To Remember:
"God Cares And He Loves You."

Share Your Testimony

God has done so much for you. If you look back over your life and seen where God has brought you from, you have to testify. We all have a Testimony because without God it could have been the other way. Write what God has done for you in your life, and start sharing your Testimony with others. "I will speak of thy testimonies also before kings, and will not be ashamed" (Psalm 119:46 KJV)

Write Your Testimony (s)

_____
_____
_____
_____
_____
_____
_____
_____
_____
_____
_____
_____
_____
_____
_____
_____
_____
_____
_____
_____

Been Released

I Will Overcome Be Strong And Keep On Keeping On

God is Reviving, Restoring, Refreshing, & Renewing you, so you are able to see what God see's in you. God created you, so He knows what you can do! Trust and have Faith in God and He will give you the Confidence to Walk in Your Purpose!
~Stay Encouraged~
Keisha "Been Released" Wade

Dear _____,
      (Your Name)

It's your time to be elevated, as you "Take A Leap Of Faith", and Trust God Because He Is taking you to your next level! The next Words of Encouragement will encourage you to *"Take A Leap Of Faith"* with confidence that God has Gifted you to do. This is also a workbook guide with sessions that will give you ways to stay encouraged and to operate in your Gift.

I Decree and Declare and Speak into your life that God Is About To Promote You Higher In Many Different Ways. Continue To "Put Your Faith and Trust In Him As You "Take A Leap Of Faith", Because When You Take This Leap Of Faith You Will See the Power Of God Take You Places You Have Never Seen or Been Before. "But as it is written, Eye hath no seen, nor ear heard, neither have entered into the heart of man, the things which God hath prepared for them that love him" (1st Corinthians 2:9 KJV). Get Ready God Is About To Deliver You, Your Good News!

Stay Encouraged,

    Keisha "Been Released" Wade

CHAPTER 5

Seek God First

"But seek ye first the kingdom of God, and his righteousness;
and all these things shall be added unto you."
(Matthew 6:33 KJV)

Always Seek God in everything you do. The Word of God say's "But seek ye first the kingdom of God, and his righteousness, and all these things shall be added unto you" (Matthew 6:33 KJV). When you seek God first and stay in His presence you are allowing Him to lead and guide you to your next level. Continue to Pray and know what God's Purpose is for you. Listen to the Holy Spirit as He Speaks, because He will lead and guide you in how to get prepared, so He can position you to what He has planned for you in your life. It's time for you to step out of your comfort level and have the Faith to do what God has already birth in you to do. Are You Ready to Go to Your Next Level?

Remember You were Designed with an Unstoppable Spirit!! There are going to be so many surprises God has in store for you as you step into a New Season of Life. You have been Promoted, and God is going to Change Your Status of where you are Right Now!! It's Your Elevation Time, so take that Leap of Faith and see where the Mighty Power of God takes you!!! Everyone has a Purpose in their Life, and even thou there are some trials, some tribulations, some up's and some down's that you have experienced, don't let that stop you from doing what God has Planned for You! Some of the things that you went through was Only God Preparing You for Your Purpose in Life! God is Birthing Businesses, Ministries, Entrepreneurship, and so many great things in you. God is at this very moment Elevating You to Your Next Blessings, Your Next Levels and Your Next Purpose in Your Life.

This is Your Season to step out on Faith and do what God has instructed You to Do! Start opening the doors of opportunities that God has for you, because You will never know what God has Blessed you with if You do not open the Door! You have to Grow, do not continue to stay where you are year after year, there is a Blessing in your Faith Walk, and it's going to be greater than you could ever imagine! ~Stay Encouraged~

Released Encouragement Thought To Remember:
"Keep God First In Your Life."

Four Biblical Principles
The Power Of God In Your
Prayer, Purpose, Preparation, and Positioning

Prayer- Ask, Seek, Knock. Let God know that you're asking for direction, seeking His will, and knocking on the door that God has already said is yours. Claim His promise to give to those who ask, reveal to those who seek, and open to those who knock. (Matthew 7:7-8 KJV) "Continue to pray, the Word of God says in (Mark 11:24 NIV) "Therefore I tell you, whatever you ask for in prayer, believe that you have received it, and it will be yours".

What Are You Asking, Seeking, Knocking And Praying To God For?

_____
_____
_____
_____
_____
_____
_____
_____
_____
_____
_____
_____

Four Biblical Principles

The Power of God In Your Prayer, Purpose, Preparation, and Positioning

Purpose- God's Purpose Is The One That Will Last.
"Many are the plans in a person's heart, but it is the Lord's purpose that prevails" (Proverbs 19:21 NIV) and (Jeremiah 29:11 NIV) "For I know the plans I have for you, declares the Lord, plans to prosper you and not to harm you, plans to give you hope and a future."

What Is Your Purpose?

_____
_____
_____
_____
_____
_____
_____
_____
_____
_____
_____
_____
_____
_____

Four Biblical Principles
The Power of God In Your
Prayer, Purpose, Preparation, and Positioning

Preparation- Start Preparing To Do The Work.

Ephesians 4:12 (NIV) "To equip his people for works of service, so that the body of Christ may be built up."

God Is Speaking To You, Listen To His Voice, And Follow His Instructions. How Are You Going To Start Preparing?

_____
_____
_____
_____
_____
_____
_____
_____
_____
_____
_____
_____
_____
_____
_____
_____

Four Biblical Principles
The Power of God In Your
Prayer, Purpose, Preparation, and Positioning

Positioning- God Is Directing You. Matthew 6:33(AMP) "But first *and* most importantly seek (aim at, strive after) His kingdom and His righteousness [His way of doing and being right the attitude and character of God], and all these things will be given to you also."

Where Is God Leading, Guiding, And Directing You?

_____
_____
_____
_____
_____
_____
_____
_____
_____
_____
_____
_____
_____
_____
_____

CHAPTER 6

Do It With Confidence

"Therefore do not throw away your confidence, which has a great reward. For you have need of endurance, so that when you have done the will of God you may receive what is promised."
(Hebrews 10:35-36 ESV)

I Decree and Declare that at this very moment, God is Healing you from feeling broken, hurt, lost, empty, depress, overwhelmed, stressed, and how ever you may be feeling at this moment. God is releasing everything, and setting you free to become the Confident Person You need to be. In order for you to do what God has purposed in your life to do, you have to be healed, delivered, and set free from it. God wants to use you to be able to show others how the Power of God Works in your life, because if others see what God has done in your life then they can believe that God can do it in their lives. Whatever God has given you the ability to do, do it with having Faith, Trust, and Confidence in God. You will get through it, and it will be accomplished because God is in the midst of it all. No matter how you may feel, God say's you are going to get through this because He Has a Purpose, and He Has Plans for you. So, do not throw your confidence away because it has a great reward, and as you are obedient to God you will receive your promises that He has promised you. There were so many things that you went through, and there are somethings that you are going through right now. I want to encourage you and let you know that God will take your broken pieces and give you a Brand-New Start. This is your year of feeling Renewed, Refreshed, Revived, and Restored, because God is setting you free and Releasing you from every shackle, chain, generational curses, hurt, pain, stress, depression, suicidal thoughts, relationships, your health and anything that's trying to hold you back from being set Free. I ask you this question, How do you feel about yourself? Strip away your title or role you are in life. What does your *"Confident Facial Expression"* look like? We all have some type of facial expression worn on our face whether it's emotional, physically, and spiritually. Some of the expressions that's shown on our face is: fear, doubt, frustration, anger, sadness, happiness, joy, etc.... People can tell how you may feel by looking at your facial expression. It's time to change the way you are feeling, thinking, and acting about yourself. God's desire is for You to become "Strong, Healed, Bold, Confident, Loved, Delivered, Set Free and Successful, along with other positive characteristics.

I want to encourage you today to be confident in all the things that God has given you the ability to do. No matter where you start, you can have a Great Finish! Decide today to do something great for God and Yourself. Even thou you may be going through a situation; God can still raise you up and do great and mighty things in you and through you! Start speaking positive words into the atmosphere and allow God to show and teach you how to take authority with confidence of the situation. You must continue to push to your purpose that God has planned for you. The Word of God say's in Jeremiah 29:11 KJV "For I know the thoughts that I think toward you, says the Lord, thoughts of peace and not of evil, to give you a future and hope". God knows that you can do it, because He put it in you to do. Whenever you start to think that you can't, or something is not going to go right you must renew your mind, in Romans 12:1-2 KJV it says "I beseech you therefore, brethren, by the mercies of God, that ye present your bodies a living sacrifice, holy, acceptable unto God, which is your reasonable service. And be not conformed to this world: but be ye transformed by the renewing of your mind, that ye may prove what is that good, and acceptable, and perfect, will of God". There are so many Great Blessings that God is about to do in your life, and the elevation He is about to take you to. It states in 1st Corinthians 2:9 KJV "But as it is written, Eye hath not seen, nor ear heard, neither have entered into the heart of man, the things which God hath prepared for them that love him". Start focusing on the things that are going to take you to your next level.

God's Word say's in Isaiah 43:18-19 "Do not remember the former things behold, I am going a New Thing...", and if God can make a way in the wildness, and rivers in the desert, He can make a way for you! Don't look back and be ashamed, but look forward and start enjoying the Life that

God wants you to have while Living it with Confidence! God has Blessed You with Many Gifts, so do not be afraid to use them. God did not give you the spirit of fear............(2nd Timothy 1:7), so be CONFIDENT, when using your GIFTS that GOD has BLESSED You with, because Your Gifts will make room for you and bring you before Great men.... (Proverbs 18:16). Don't worry about what it looks like, or what it use to be, but Accept what God says it's going to be. Put ALL Your Confidence, Trust, and Faith in God because the same way God did it for you before, He will make a way for you this time and Forever more! God says with the Faith the Size of a Mustard Seed He will move mountains (Matthew 17:20). I Decree and Declare that New Things are going to start happening, and God is going to Perform a Miracle in Your Life, Marriage, Health, Finances, Employment, New Home, Family and what you stand in need of.

God is Preparing You for Great Things, so that means that some things will change and shift in your life. God will Override the enemy's plans, so do not look at how far you've got to go, but look where God has brought you from, and look where God is bringing you to! The enemy cannot touch what God says is His and what God says it's Yours!! Although You may be going through a Transition right now, keep your head held high, because the more the enemy try to come up against you, the more You need to Give God the Praise because He Just Cancelled the enemy's plans. "He troubles the plans of those who try to fool people, so that their hands cannot do what they plan." (Job 5:12 NLV). The enemy must not know who our father is. It's Time For You to Start Enjoying Your Life! You have done so much for others, and Now It's Time For You To Do For You. It's time for You to Accomplish Your Vision, Dreams, Goals, and Purpose in YOUR LIFE. Don't let fear talk you out of it, take that leap of faith, and step into the unknown. God will Always Lead and Guide you into the Right Direction as You begin to Follow Him. As you go through this Journey taking Many Leaps of Faith you will step into New Levels that Will Lead You into Great Beginnings, Miracles, Favor, Increase, and Success! God is speaking to you to "Step Out On Faith", because that One Step of Faith Will Cause Your Life to Change for the Better. Don't worry about the "What if's", Focus on "It Is So", and begin to step into the unknown to fulfill God's Destiny that will Lead and Guide You to Accomplish Your Vision, Dreams, Goals, and Purpose In YOUR LIFE!

I Decree and Declare and Speak into the atmosphere that you will walk in Victory, you will walk with Confidence, and God is going to Release the Promises to come into Your Life. Blessings after Blessings, Miracles after Miracles Expect Them Every Day! Here comes your Favor, Joy, Peace, Faith, Job, Car, House, Healing, Deliverance, Breakthrough, Wealth, Restoration, Love, Happiness, Forgiveness, New Opportunities, New Beginnings, A New

Way of Living, and Everything that you stand in need of. You have Spoken them into the Atmosphere and Obeyed the Voice of God, and now you shall have your BLESSINGS that God has Promised to give to You. Enjoy your Blessings because more will be coming, In Jesus Name Amen (Deuteronomy 28: 1-6). God has Blessed You with Many Gifts, so have the confidence to know that with God you can do All things through Christ that strengthens you (Philippians 4:13). I want to encourage you to Continue to Be Bold, Strong, Confident, and Courageous. Wherever God leads you to go, and whatever God tells you to do, You Will Be Successful! ~Stay Encouraged~

Released Encouragement Thought To Remember:
"You Can, You Will, & You Shall Do
What God has Equipped You to Do."

It's Time For You To Start Focusing And Pushing To Your Purpose That God Has For You!

1. *What* are the things that you need to start focusing on that's going to take you to your next level?

   _____
   _____
   _____
   _____

2. *How* are you going to start focusing on the things that's going to take you to your next level?

   _____
   _____
   _____
   _____

3. *When* are you going to start focusing on the things that's going to take you to your next level?

   _____
   _____
   _____
   _____

What Is God's Desire For You?

God's desire is for _____ to be _____
                          (Your Name)   **(My Purpose)**

Define These Terms:
Confident, Confidence, Vision, Purpose, Level, Attitude, Faith

Confident: To feel, believe, and show that you can do something well and having the confidence to succeed.

Scripture: Philippians 4:13 KJV- "I can do all things through Christ which strengtheneth me"

What does *Confident* mean to you?

_____

_____

Confidence: A feeling and belief of being certain that something will happen, as you show it in your action.

Scripture: -Philippians 1:6 ESV- "And I am sure of this, that he who began a good work in you will bring it to completion at the day of Jesus Christ."

What does *Confidence* mean to you?

_____

_____

Vision: The ability to see and plan the future with wisdom.

Scripture: Habakkuk 2:2 KJV- "And the LORD answered me, and said, Write the vision, and make it plain upon tables, that he may run that readeth it."

What does *Vision* mean to you?

_____

_____

Purpose: The reason for which something is created and done.

Scripture: Job 42:2 NET- "I know that you can do all things; no purpose of yours can be thwarted".

What does *Purpose* mean to you?

_____

_____

Level: To rise and attain the position God has planned.

Scripture: Psalm 32:8 AMP- "I will instruct you and teach you in the way you should go; I will counsel you [who are willing to learn] with My eye upon you."

What does *Level* mean to you?

_____

_____

Attitude: A feeling or a way of thinking that can and will affect a person's thoughts, words, and behavior.

Scripture: Ephesians 4:23-24 AMP- "And be continually renewed in the spirit of your mind [having a fresh, untarnished mental and spiritual attitude], and put on the new self [the regenerated and renewed nature], created in God's image, [godlike] in the righteousness and holiness of the truth [living in a way that expresses to God your gratitude for your salvation]".

What does *Attitude* mean to you?

_____

_____

Faith: Believing and Trusting in God that it's already done.

Scripture: Hebrews 11:1 KJV- "Now faith is the substance of things hoped for, the evidenced of things not seen."

What does *Faith* mean to you?

_____

_____

STAY FOCUS:
Matthew 14:22-33 KJV

Jesus Walks on the Water

"Immediately he made the disciples get into the boat and go before him to the other side, while he dismissed the crowds. And after he had dismissed the crowds, he went up on the mountain by himself to pray. When evening came, he was there alone, but the boat by this time was a long way from the land, beaten by the waves, for the wind was against them. And in the fourth watch of the night he came to them, walking on the sea. But when the disciples saw him walking on the sea, they were terrified, and said, "It is a ghost!" and they cried out in fear. But immediately Jesus spoke to them, saying, "Take heart; it is I. Do not be afraid.""

"And Peter answered him, "Lord, if it is you, command me to come to you on the water." He said, "Come." So Peter got out of the boat and walked on the water and came to Jesus. But when he saw the wind, he was afraid, and beginning to sink he cried out, "Lord, save me." Jesus immediately reached out his hand and took hold of him, saying to him, "O you of little faith, why did you doubt?" And when they got into the boat, the wind ceased. And those in the boat worshiped him, saying, "Truly you are the Son of God.""

God is speaking to you, and He is telling you to do something. Do not be afraid, because God is with you every step of the way. As you read the story of Jesus walking on water (Matthew 14:22-33), What is God speaking to you to do? When are you going to "Take A Leap Of Faith", and do what God has Purposed in your heart to do?

_____
_____
_____
_____
_____
_____
_____
_____
_____
_____
_____
_____
_____
_____
_____
_____
_____
_____
_____
_____
_____

CHAPTER 7

Characteristics Of Being Confident

"Not only that, but we rejoice in our sufferings, knowing that suffering produces endurance, and endurance produces character, and character produces hope, and hope does not put us to shame, because God's love has been poured into our hearts through the Holy Spirit who has been given to us."
(Romans 5:3-5 ESV)

You are Confident and you have the characteristics that go along with it. Do you see yourself as God sees you, because God sees you Strong, more than a Conqueror, a Go-Getter and Successful in life? Everyone has a Purpose in their Life, and even thou there are some trials and some tribulations, some up's and some down's that you have experienced, don't let that stop you from doing what God has Planned and Purposed for You! Everything that you went through was Only God Preparing You for Your Purpose in Life! Your Purpose has been Birth in you, and all you have to do is Allow God to use what He's Birth in you to come out, so it can be a Blessing to You and Others. God has Birth Ministries, Businesses, Inventions, Entrepreneurship, and the list goes on. Not only has God Birth Many Great Things Inside you, but God is Elevating You to Your Next Blessings, He Is Elevating You to Your Next Level and He's Elevating You to Your Next Purpose in Life. This is Your Season to Step out on Faith, and do what God has Instructed You to Do! Start opening the Doors of Opportunities that God has for you, because You will never know what God has Blessed you with if You do not open the door! You have to GROW, do not continue to stay where you are year after year, there is a Blessing in your Faith Walk, and it's going to be greater than you could ever imagine! Continue to have Positive and Healthy Thinking Only. Your Thoughts will become your Words, and your Words will become your Actions! No matter what you go through in life always remember to keep God First, and continue to be confident in all the things that God has given you the ability to do. You must see yourself as God sees you, and you will know that you are valuable, you have worth, you are gifted, you are talented, you are more than a conqueror, you have a great future, and something good is going to happen to you, because you have a Purpose!~Stay Encouraged~

Released Encouragement Thought To Remember:
"Living God's Purpose For My Life &
Becoming Confident In Who I Am."

10 Characteristics Of Being Confident

~You Put God First- Matthew 6:33 KJV- "But seek ye first the kingdom of God, and his righteousness; and all these things shall be added unto you."

~You Pray- Jeremiah 33:3 KJV- "Call unto me, and I will answer thee, and show thee great and mighty things, which thou knowest not."

~You Know Your Purpose- Romans 8:28 KJV- "And we know that all things work together for good to them that love God, to them who are the called according to his purpose."

~You Believe In Yourself- Philippians 4:13 KJV- "I can do all things through Christ which strengtheneth me."

~You Never Give Up- Galatians 6:9 KJV- "And let us not be weary in well doing: for in due season we shall reap, if we faint not."

10 Characteristics Of Being Confident

~You Are Gifted- Proverbs 18:16 KJV- "A man's gift maketh room for him, and bringeth him before great men."

~You Promote a Positive Mindset- Philippians 4:8 KJV- "Finally, brethren, whatsoever things are true, whatsoever things are honest, whatsoever things are just, whatsoever things are pure, whatsoever things are lovely, whatsoever things are of good report; if there be any virtue, and if there be any praise, think on these things."

~You Set Goals- Habakkuk 2:2 KJV- "And the Lord answered me, and said, Write the vision, and make it plain upon tables, that he may run that readeth it."

~You Take Action- Proverbs 16:3 GNT- "Ask the Lord to bless your plans, and you will be successful in carrying them out."

~You Invest In Yourself- Colossians 3:23-24 GNT- "Whatever you do, work at it with all your heart, as though you were working for the Lord and not for people.
  Remember that the Lord will give you as a reward what he has kept for his people. For Christ is the real Master you serve."

How Do You Put Your Characteristics Of Being Confident Into Action?

1. You Put God First: How & why do you put God First?

_____
_____
_____

2. You Pray: What is your prayer to God?

_____
_____
_____

3. You Know Your Purpose: What is your Purpose?

_____
_____
_____

4. You Believe In Yourself: What do you know and believe that you can do?

_____
_____
_____

5. You Never Give Up: What are some things that you say or do that keep you from giving up?

_____
_____
_____

6. You Are Gifted: What are the things that you are gifted in doing?

_____
_____
_____

7. You Promote a Positive Mindset: What do you say or do that promotes you to have a healthy positive mindset?

_____
_____
_____

8. You Set Goals: What goals do you want to accomplish?

_____
_____
_____

9. You Take Action: How do you prepare to take action?

_____
_____
_____

10. You Invest In Yourself: How do you invest in yourself?

_____
_____
_____

List and describe other characteristics of how to be confident in what God has purposed in your heart to do.

_____
_____
_____
_____
_____
_____
_____
_____
_____
_____

CHAPTER 8

Believe Like and Enjoy Yourself

"So God created man in his own image, in the image of God created he him; male and female created he them. And God saw everything that he had made, and, behold, it was very good. And the evening and the morning were the sixth day."
(Genesis 1:27 & 31 KJV)

To enjoy who God created you to be it starts with You. You have to like and love yourself, enjoy who you are, and accept how God created you. That means you are unique and different from others, because God has something special inside of you that He wants to shine through you. One of the things that you must continue to do is "Start Speaking Positive Words about Yourself into the Atmosphere" in Proverbs 18:21 KJV it states, "Death and life are in the power of the tongue, and they that love it shall eat the fruit thereof". What type of words are you speaking? What type of thinking are you thinking? Your thoughts will become your words, and your words will become your action, and what you believe you will start to see and do. See yourself as God see's you. Start seeing, believing, and doing the Vision that God has given you and you will see your Life Change. Continue to keep speaking what God says you are, and who God says you will be. Although in life you may have faced some trials and some tribulations, I Want To Encourage And Say To You, "Do Not Give Up", because God Will Use You To Do Great And Mighty Things. God will equip and help you to overcome areas that you have challenges in to bring forth

His messages, miracles, testimony's through you. The Bible says in 1st Corinthians 1:27 NLT "Instead, God chose things the world considers foolish in order to shame those who think they are wise, and He chose things that are powerless to shame those who are powerful", so I ask the question why not you? Did you know that you were chosen by God to be the one to stand out, so if God Chose you then that means He knows that you can do it. In 1st Peter 2:9 TLB it states "But you are not like that, for you have been chosen by God himself — you are priests of the King, you are holy and pure, you are God's very own. All this so that you may show to others how God called you out of darkness into his wonderful light". What's holding you back from doing or being the person that God has instilled in you to become? Allow God to mold you into what He wants you to be, and not what family, friends or others want you to be. Your Worth and Value is not what you are, but who you are in Christ Jesus. Once again it starts with you, and once you learn to accept, come to peace and believe in yourself, start saying "I am going to Believe in myself, and I am going to Enjoy who God created me to be, I will succeed in life, and I will see myself as God sees me, my life will start to change and this change will affect my life for the better." Remember to believe that you are valuable and precious in God's eye sight (Isaiah 43:4 GNT). If you take a couple of seconds and look into your heart, how do you feel about yourself?. If your answer doesn't agree with God's Words, I encourage you to begin today renewing your mind about yourself it states in Romans 12:1-2 KJV "I beseech you therefore, brethren, by the mercies of God, that ye present your bodies a living sacrifice, holy, acceptable unto God, which is your reasonable service. And be not conformed to this world: but be ye transformed by the renewing of your mind, that ye may prove what is that good, acceptable, and perfect, will of God." When you have a renewed mind, you are able to think more clearly, so I pray that you open up your ears that you may hear the Voice of God speaking to you, and I pray that you open up your eyes that you see where God is directing you. God has given you so many gifts specifically just for you! God wouldn't have given you those gifts, abilities, interests, talents, your personality, and life's turning points unless He intended to use them for His Glory. God has birth so many opportunities in you such as Ministry, becoming an Author, Inventing new things, Owning Your Own business, Creating New Ideas, Being A Designer, and the list goes on. You have to start believing and confessing what God says, because He gave you those gifts so He knows that you can do it. God's Word states that you can, because in Philippians 4:13 KJV it says, "I can do all things through Christ which strengtheneth me". Remember God created you with a "Purpose", and in Psalm 139:14 NIV it says "I praise you because I am fearfully and wonderfully made; your works are wonderful, I know that full well". ~Stay Encouraged~

Released Encouragement Thought To Remember:
"I Love Me Some Me."

4 Principles To Believe Like and Enjoy Yourself:

1. Speak Great Things About Yourself -Declare and Decree who God says you are!! You are not a mistake, God is for you and He loves you. Speak positive words about yourself into the atmosphere.

Isaiah 55:11 KJV- "So shall my word be that goeth forth out of my mouth: it shall not return unto me void, but it shall accomplish that which I please, and it shall prosper in the thing whereto I sent it."

2. Refrain From Comparing Yourself With Others- God created you to look, to be, and to do things differently. When looking at how others are, just look to the people that God has placed in your life, and certain people as good examples to follow (mentors, leaders, etc..).

Galatians 6:4 TLB "Let everyone be sure that he is doing his very best, for then he will have the personal satisfaction of work well done and won't need to compare himself with someone else."

4 Principles To Believe Like and Enjoy Yourself:

3. Focus On Your Reachable Abilities Instead Of Limitations- Don't allow yourself to concentrate so much on your weakness or challenges. If you are going to focus on it, make it an effort to turn your weakness or challenges into strengths. Say, "God show me how I can turn this weakness or challenge into a strength". Focus on what you can do, and God will show you, and give you directions on how to overcome anything that's limiting you.

Ephesians 3:20 NKJV "Now to Him who is able to do exceedingly abundantly above all that we ask or think, according to the power that works in us."

4. You Must Continue To Believe In God And Yourself- You can't feel that you are lacking anything or there is anything wrong with you! God will never anoint you to be anyone other than yourself. God is proud of who He made you to be, so you need to continue to go forward, and be who God created you to be.

Philippians 4:13 KJV "I can do all things through Christ which strengtheneth me"

CHAPTER 9

Remember Your Dream Vision and Purpose

"Remember ye not, that, when I was yet with you,
I told you these things?"
(2nd Thessalonians 2:5 KJV)

There are some things in your life that God has given you a dream and a vision about, and as of today you haven't started it or you haven't finished it. You must have confidence in everything that God has given you the ability to do. God is saying two things 1. You must start it. 2. You must finish it. The vision that God has birthed in you, will Bless you in many ways, but when are you going to start it or finish it? You have the Faith that it can be done, and even thou you have Faith you have to have works. The bible talks about Faith without works in dead. God has already Birth it through you, but why are you holding back? Is it because of Fear, Doubt, Responsibility, Failure, Rejection etc..? God is saying why are you holding back?

The word of God says in Philippians 4:13 KJV, "I can do all things through Christ which strengthen me". God is saying Remember what I told you, Remember what I showed you. When God gives you a vision and your purpose for your life you need to write the Vision, make it Plain and run with it (Habakkuk 2:2). Whatever God tells you to do, do it with Passion, and do it to the Glory of

God. Sometimes you may not see a way for your vision to come to pass. The Bible says, The vision is yet for an appointed time, wait for it because it will surely come….Habakkuk 2:3. You may not know how to get from where you are today, but God does, that's why you must seek him in everything. If you do not know what your vision or purpose is, ask God and He will reveal it to you. God will lead you to your next step, vision, and purpose, and as God is doing that have the Confidence to know that you can do it too. Whatever God tells you to do, He will equip you, and He will fulfill the vision He has placed in your heart. God already sees you doing it, but you must see yourself doing it too, because the more you see yourself doing your vision and knowing your purpose the sooner it will become a Reality.

Before a Vision is clear God shows you a glimpse of it, it's just like a picture developing you see something here and there, you may not see the full picture or you may see the full picture finished, but you must start where God tells you to start to bring it to completion. God is speaking to you and He's saying that, It's going to take work, but you must stay Focus, and not allow yourself to get distracted. You want to see the Vision Fully come to pass. You have been Praying for this to happen! I want to encourage you to take your Vision and Run with it, because when you do that God is going to take you to the Next Level! Continue to seek God on every decision and every plan that you start to do, and watch what God will do through you. God is going to use you in that Vision and Purpose that He has given you to bring others to Christ! So, remember what God has spoken to you there may be some up's and some downs but remember Given up is not an option, continue to Believe and have Faith because God has given you the Opportunity to Experience so much More!!! ~Stay Encouraged~

Released Encouragement Thought To Remember:
"I Will Pursue, Overtake and Recover My Purpose."

Remember Your Dream Vision and Purpose

"But as it is written, Eye hath not seen, nor ear heard, neither have entered into the heart of man, the things which God hath prepared for them for them that love him." (1st Corinthians 2:9 KJV)

What Is Your Dream Vision and Purpose?

1. What is your Dream, Vision, and Purpose that God has shown or told you?

_____
_____
_____

2. What do you need to get started?

_____
_____
_____

3. What do you need to finish it?

_____
_____
_____

CHAPTER 10

It's Not Over
"And though you started with little,
you will end with much"
(Job 8:7 NLT)

God is so Amazing! I want to encourage you to let you know that what God has for you it's for you, and what God says you are going to do you will do it. So, do not give up because God Will Provide! You have a Purpose in Life and guess what It's Not Over For You. Do not allow the enemy to have control over you, and try to tell you that you can't, because God is removing fear, doubt, frustration, and the feeling of being overwhelmed, and Replacing it with Boldness, Strength, Peace, and being Confident. Whatever God brings you to, he will have you do it. "For God hath not given us the spirit of fear; but of power, and of love, and of a sound mind" (2nd Timothy 1:7 KJV). Start speaking life, and watch the mighty Power of God Work in Your life. You have done so much for others, and Now God is saying, "IT'S YOUR TIME"! That's why God has a "SERIES" of INCREASE, BLESSINGS, FAVOR etc.. that's coming into your Life! Meaning, God has a Number of Things, Many People, and Different Events that will Bless You One After Another! God is saying, "Don't Give Up, Soon You Will Be Walking In Your Season of "OVERFLOW"!!! You have a purpose in life, and although there were somethings that have happened in your life, do not allow "IT" to be the reason you lose focus on your purpose. Do not look at where you are at this moment, but Focus and Trust God in where He is going to take you to. God says that "It's Not Over". Where you are right now you can still operate and do your purpose. Whatever God has Gifted You to do or Purposed in your Heart you can still do it. You have too much ahead to be looking at what was behind you. It's time to Reconnect to your passion, to discover your new Life Purpose, Set Realistic Goals, and Empower Yourself with a Plan for Your Future. When you do this you have to Embrace Change! Although it may seem challenging, Stay Encouraged, because with God anything is possible all you have to do is Believe (Mark 9:23). When you do this change you are going to be taking on Your Life with a Purpose, a New Look, a Better Feeling, an Awesome Attitude, and Determination in walking in your Purpose. ~Stay Encouraged~

Released Encouragement Thought To Remember:
"This Is Just The Beginning Of A Brand New You."

IT'S NOT OVER BECAUSE YOU WILL……

Uncover New Opportunities- God will give you the experience to discover New Opportunities, New Blessings, New Connections, and New Beginnings.

Reawaken Lost Goals- Remember the things that you wanted to do, but you haven't finished them. You might even say or think "I haven't even started them", but you have started it, because God showed you that vision, and you thought about it. There's been many times that you've though about it, and even visualized yourself doing it. Start remembering the things that you have a Passion for, and start reaching and completing your goals.

Create New Paths- Have you been taking the same paths year after year? Start "Taking a Leap of Faith" in a new direction, by committing to God, and allowing God to lead and guide you towards new ways of accomplishing what you want to do.

Redesign Your Future- Question? "Are you working on your life or are you just in it"? What plan(s) did God reveal, show, and tell you to start doing to build towards your future? As you build towards your future listen to the instructions of God.

I Declare I Am Poem

I Declare I Am....

I shall have what I Decree. I Shall have what I Declare, I Shall have what I Believe, and I Shall have what I Speak into My Own Life, knowing what God has Promised Me it is for Me!
"Delight yourself in the Lord, and he will give you the desires of your heart"
(Psalm 37:4ESV)

I Declare I am Successful, I Declare I am Healed
I Declare I am Blessed, I Declare I am Delivered
I Declare I am Wealthy, I Declare I am Gifted
I Declare I am a Testimony
I Declare I am an Overcomer
I Declare I am Going where God leads Me
I Declare I am born with an Unstoppable Spirit
I Declare I am Covered by the Blood of Jesus Christ
I Declare I am Confident, Bold, & more than a Conqueror
I Declare I am Strong and will be nobody else but ME!
~Stay Encouraged~
By: Keisha "Been Released" Wade

Receiving Christ In Your Life

1. **Confess you are a sinner.**
(Romans 5:12 & Romans 5:23)

2. **Ask for forgiveness and Repent from your sins.**
(Luke 13:5)

3. **Ask Jesus to come into your life and be your savior.**
(John 3:15, Romans 5:8, Romans 10:9)

4. **When you talk to God you are praying.**

Here is a prayer asking Jesus to come into your life.

Dear God, I admit that I am a sinner and I need forgiveness, I believe that Jesus Christ shed His precious blood and died for my sins. I believe that He rose on the third day and I invite Jesus Christ to come into my heart and life as my personal Savior.

~Amen~

The Benediction

May The LORD bless you and keep you;
the LORD make his face shine on you
and be gracious to you; The LORD turn his face toward
you and give you peace.

Numbers 6:24-26 NIV

About the Author Keisha "Been Released" Wade

Keisha "Been Released" Wade is a Woman of God (WOG) who is an Inspirational Encouragement Speaker, Author, Purpose & Transformation Life Coach, and Prayer Warrior. God has given her a Ministry called Released which is an Encouragement Ministry to pray, uplift, encourage, and empower others. God has given her the Gift of Encouragement where she Speaks and Write to Uplift others She shares her Testimony of how God lead her to overcome many challenges, asking for forgiveness, and coming into Victory! She is a Woman of God that Loves the Lord, and she is a willing vessel that wants to be used by God to help Build the Kingdom of God Up! Her favorite quote is "My Past Will Be A Testimony For My Future".

Contact Information:

Keisha "Been Released" Wade

www.beenreleased.com

Follow me on:

Instagram: @keishabeenreleased

Facebook: Keisha "Been Released" Wade

Been Released

Keisha "Been Released" Wade

Keisha "Been Released" Wade

Made in the USA
Middletown, DE
05 June 2021